CHRISTMAS ON A PLATE

CHRISTMAS ON A PLATE

Emma Marsden

SQUARE PEG

Published by Square Peg 2014

10 9 8 7 6 5 4 3 2 1

First published in Great Britain in 2014 by
Square Peg
Random House, 20 Vauxhall Bridge Road,
London SW1V 2SA
www.vintage-books.co.uk

Addresses for companies within The Random House Group
Limited can be found at:
www.randomhouse.co.uk/offices.htm
The Random House Group Limited Reg. No. 954009

A CIP catalogue record for this book is available from the
British Library

ISBN 978 0 224 10101 1

The Random House Group Limited supports The Forest
Stewardship Council (FSC®), the leading international
forest certification organisation. Our books carrying the
FSC® label are printed on FSC® certified paper. FSC is the
only forest certification scheme endorsed by the leading
environmental organisations, including Greenpeace.
Our paper procurement policy can be found at www.
randomhouse.co.uk/environment

Mixed Sources
Product group from well-managed
forests and other controlled sources
www.fsc.org Cert no. TT-COC-2139
© 1996 Forest Stewardship Council
FSC

Photography by Sarah Cuttle
Food styling by Emma Marsden, Ellie Jarvis and Alice Whiting

Typeset and designed by Anna Green
at www.siulendesign.com

Printed and bound in Italy by L.E.G.O. S.p.A.

In the same series:

HEART
ON A ♥
PLATE

This book includes some clever ways to create Christmas-themed food without requiring any specialist equipment. For many recipes, all you need is a steady hand and a couple of hours to make and craft. For some, there are brilliant shaped utensils you can buy cheaply and which you'll have for years to come to create your own festive traditions. Happy cooking!

Unless stated otherwise:
• All eggs are medium
• All spoon measurements are level
• All vegetables should be peeled

CONTENTS ❄

STAINED GLASS BISCUITS WITH A TOUCH OF SPICE

These simple biscuits are seasoned with a heady mix of rich spices. Hang them at the window to let the winter light flood through the middle.

MAKES ABOUT 12

a little oil, for greasing
110g unsalted butter, softened
40g golden caster sugar, plus extra for
  sprinkling
1 tbsp golden syrup
200g plain flour, plus extra for dusting
1 tsp bicarbonate of soda
½ tsp ground ginger
½ tsp mixed spice
½ tsp ground cloves
a pinch of salt
1 bag of coloured boiled sweets
edible glue

You will need
a set of Christmas-shaped biscuit cutters

Preheat oven to 180°C/160°C fan/gas 4. Oil a baking sheet well.

Beat together the butter, sugar and golden syrup until smooth. Sift over the flour, bicarbonate of soda and all the spices with the salt. Mix well again until all the dry ingredients are incorporated into the butter mixture. At this stage you may need to bring the mixture together with your hands. Knead lightly to make a smooth dough. Shape into a disc then wrap in cling film and chill for 15 minutes.

Roll out half the dough between two sheets of cling film until 3mm thick. Stamp out the shapes using the biscuit cutters, rerolling the dough as necessary. Cut out holes from the middle, leaving at least a 1.5cm border. Transfer to the baking sheet, then push a skewer into the top to make a hole. Do the same with the remaining dough.

STAINED GLASS BISCUITS CONTINUED

Bash each sweet, still in its wrapper, using a pestle and mortar, until it's finely crushed. Sprinkle one crushed sweet inside each hole and bake for 15–20 minutes. Transfer to a wire rack to cool.

If you want to decorate the biscuits, brush a little edible glue all over each one and sprinkle with caster sugar. Allow to set before hanging.

CANDY CANE BISCUITS

Twisting two different-coloured biscuit doughs together and shaping one end gently into a hook creates these pretty biscuits. If you want to get ahead they'll keep in an airtight container for up to a week.

MAKES 6

For the vanilla dough
30g butter, at room temperature
30g caster sugar
1 tsp vanilla extract
60g plain flour

For the red dough
½ tsp red food paste, such as claret
½ tsp vanilla extract
30g butter, at room temperature
30g caster sugar
60g plain flour

To finish
1 medium egg white
golden caster sugar, for sprinkling

Make the vanilla dough by beating the butter, sugar and vanilla extract together in a bowl. Slowly add the flour, continuing to beat to incorporate it all. Bring the mixture together with your hands to make a dough, adding a drizzle of water if necessary, then wrap in cling film and chill for 15 minutes.

To make the red biscuit dough, stir together the red food paste and vanilla extract in a bowl. Add the butter and sugar and beat together to make a paste, add the flour and mix, then knead as before. Wrap and chill for 15 minutes.

Line a baking sheet with baking parchment. Preheat the oven to 180°C/160°C fan/gas 4.

Fondest Greetings
for Your Happiness

CANDY CANE BISCUITS CONTINUED

Divide each piece of dough into 6 pieces. Roll a plain piece of dough gently with your hands to make a 16cm length. Do the same with a red piece. Twist each piece around the other, then roll very carefully again to shape the dough like a rope. Shape into a candy cane with a crook at one end, then trim the top and bottom to neaten the edges. Put on the baking sheet, then brush with egg white and sprinkle with the caster sugar. Do the same with the rest of the dough to make 6 candy canes. Chill for 10 minutes.

Bake in the oven for 12–15 minutes until golden, then transfer to a wire rack to cool.

CRANBERRY AND RUM STAR CHRISTMAS TREE

A stunning sweet finale to Christmas lunch instead of the traditional pudding. The shortbread thins, made with pistachio and lemon, are sandwiched together with cranberry and rum ice cream and finished with a light dusting of icing sugar.

SERVES 6

For the ice cream
2 tbsp rum
50g dried cranberries or sour cherries
300ml full-fat Greek-style yogurt
100g golden caster sugar

For the pistachio thins
125g plain flour
25g pistachio nuts, plus 1 tbsp, finely chopped
75g unsalted butter, chilled and diced
zest of 1 lemon
40g caster sugar
1 medium egg yolk, beaten
icing sugar, for dusting

You will need
a set of different-sized star cutters

Put the rum into a small bowl and add the dried fruit. Set aside to macerate. Put the yogurt and sugar into a freezeproof container and whisk together. Freeze for 1–2 hours, until firm. Give it a good stir to break up the crystals, then stir the rum and dried fruit mixture into it and continue to freeze for around 3 hours, until hard.

Preheat the oven to 180°C/160°C fan/gas 4.

Put the flour into a food processor with the nuts and whiz until the nuts are finely chopped. Add the butter, lemon zest and caster sugar, then pulse until the mixture resembles fine breadcrumbs.

Add the egg yolk and whiz again, then tip into a bowl and knead lightly to bring the mixture together. Shape into a disc, then wrap in cling film and chill for 15 minutes.

CRANBERRY AND RUM STAR CHRISTMAS TREE CONTINUED

Roll the mixture between two sheets of baking parchment until it's about 3mm thick. Stamp out 6 stars using a 9.5cm cutter, 6 stars using a 7cm cutter, 6 stars using a 5cm cutter and 6 stars using a 3.5cm cutter, rerolling the dough as necessary.

Put the top piece of baking parchment on to a baking sheet and put the stars on top. Bake for 8–10 minutes, until golden. Transfer to a wire rack to cool.

To serve, put the largest stars on to individual plates. Top with a spoonful of the yogurt ice cream, then continue to layer the biscuits and ice cream twice more, finishing with the smallest star. Sprinkle with the chopped pistachios and dust with icing sugar.

SPICED CHEESECAKE SHOTS

A heavenly combination of crushed amaretti biscuits and spiced cheesecake mousse, decorated with a white chocolate holly leaf. If you want to prepare ahead, these will sit quite happily in the fridge for up to a day.

SERVES 8

50g white chocolate
edible iridescent green dust
50g amaretti biscuits
1 medium egg white
50g golden caster sugar
100g cream cheese
1 tsp ground ginger
½ tsp ground cinnamon
150ml double cream
a handful of blueberries

Melt the white chocolate in a bowl resting over a pan of simmering water, making sure the base doesn't touch the water. Take the bowl off the pan and allow to cool for 10–15 minutes. Line a baking sheet or board with baking parchment.

Spoon the melted chocolate into a piping bag and snip just the end. Pipe holly leaf outlines all over the parchment, around 5cm in length. Chill to set, then dust with edible iridescent green dust.

Crush the amaretti biscuits on a board with a rolling pin or in a mini food processor.

Whisk the egg white in a clean, grease-free bowl, then whisk in half the sugar. In a separate bowl, whisk the cream cheese and spices together. Gradually fold in the double cream and the remaining sugar, then finally fold in the egg white.

SPICED CHEESECAKE SHOTS CONTINUED

Spoon into a piping bag fitted with a 1cm nozzle. Spoon half the crushed amaretti into 8 shot glasses. Next, pipe the cheesecake mixture halfway up the shot glasses. Sprinkle with the remaining amaretti and pipe the remaining cheesecake mixture on top of the amaretti. Sprinkle with a little more iridescent dust, then rest one or two holly leaves on the top and finish with a couple of blueberries, brushed with a little more dust.

PEAR, MINCEMEAT AND PECAN CRACKERS

Crisp filo pastry hides a moreish fruity filling of pear, mincemeat and chopped pecan nuts, parcelled up and pinched at the end to mimic a cracker. Drizzle with golden icing, then decorate with a handful of gold 'baubles'.

SERVES 6

2 ripe pears
3 tbsp mincemeat
20g pecan nuts, toasted and chopped
zest of 1 orange
1 tsp ground mixed spice
a pinch of salt
6 sheets of filo pastry
50–75g butter, melted

To decorate
75g golden icing sugar
edible gold balls

Preheat the oven to 200°C/180°C fan/gas 6. Line a baking sheet with baking parchment.

Chop the pears into small pieces and put into a bowl with the mincemeat, pecans, orange zest and mixed spice. Add the salt and stir everything together well.

Lay one sheet of filo pastry on a board, with the shortest end in line with the horizon of the board. Brush with the butter, then spoon a sixth of the mixture along the bottom edge, about 2cm in from the left-hand edge, leaving another 2cm space on the right-hand edge.

Start to roll the pastry up from the bottom to cover the mixture and continue to roll up into a parcel. Crimp the edges to make a cracker shape. Brush well with butter again, then do the same with the rest of the filo, filling and butter.

PEAR, MINCEMEAT AND PECAN CRACKERS CONTINUED

Place on the baking sheet and bake in the oven for 12–15 minutes until golden. Leave to cool.

Mix together the icing sugar and 1 teaspoon of water in a bowl until smooth. Spoon into a piping bag fitted with a 2–3mm nozzle. Pipe the icing in a zig-zag fashion all over the main body of each cracker and push the gold balls in to decorate. Leave to set before serving.

SNOWBALL TRUFFLES

These sweet treats have a firm texture and are made by combining ground nuts and white chocolate. Use the best quality white chocolate you can find for a really good flavour.

MAKES AROUND 25

50g blanched hazelnuts
50g blanched almonds
about 5 tbsp desiccated coconut
about 3 tbsp icing sugar, plus extra for dusting
60g white chocolate
75ml double cream

Roughly chop the nuts, then put into a food processor with 3 tablespoons of coconut and 1 tablespoon of icing sugar. Pulse the mixture until the nuts are finely ground. Take care not to overwhiz, otherwise the nuts will end up oily.

Tip the nuts into a bowl, then put the white chocolate into the food processor and finely chop it. Add to the bowl of nuts.

Pour the cream into a pan and bring to the boil. Pour it over the chocolate and nut mixture and stir well. Chill for 1 hour.

Sift 2 tablespoons of icing sugar into a bowl, then stir in about 2 tablespoons of desiccated coconut.

Scoop teaspoons of the mixture up and roll in your hands to make small balls. Roll them in the coconut and icing mixture. Continue to do this until all the mixture is used up. Chill overnight again, to firm up the truffles.

Reroll in icing sugar if the truffles need a dusting, then chill in an airtight container and enjoy within a week.

COCONUT BARK CAKE

This eye-catching treat is perfect for those who aren't keen on the traditional rich fruit cake. It can be made and frozen up to a month ahead, then thawed and decorated in time for Christmas Day.

SERVES 10

4 medium beetroots
175g butter, at room temperature, plus extra
  for greasing
175g golden caster sugar
3 medium eggs, beaten
150g plain flour
2 tsp baking powder
50g cocoa powder
50g dark chocolate, finely grated
2 tbsp milk

For the buttercream icing
125g butter, at room temperature
325g icing sugar
1 tbsp white rum

For the white chocolate bark
250g white chocolate, broken into pieces
desiccated coconut, for sprinkling

You will need
a 16cm round cake tin

Don rubber gloves, then peel and trim the beetroots. Put into a pan, cover with cold water and bring to the boil. Simmer for 15–20 minutes until tender. Drain and cool, then whiz in a food processor to finely chop.

Preheat the oven to 200°C/180°C fan/gas 6. Grease the cake tin and line with greaseproof paper.

Beat the butter and sugar together in a bowl until creamy. Gradually beat in the eggs, adding a little flour if the mixture looks as if it's curdling. Sift over the remaining flour, baking powder and cocoa. Add the dark chocolate and the beetroot to the bowl and fold everything together with the milk.

Spoon into the tin and bake for 50 minutes to 1 hour, until a skewer inserted into the centre comes out clean. Cool in the tin for 5 minutes, then transfer to a wire rack to cool completely.

Draw a large rectangle, around 25cm in length and 12cm in width, on a sheet of baking parchment. Turn the paper over and rest it on a board.

COCONUT BARK CAKE CONTINUED

Melt the white chocolate in a bowl resting over a pan of simmering water, making sure the base doesn't touch the water. Take the bowl off the pan and set aside to cool for 10–15 minutes. Spoon on to the rectangle, then sprinkle over the coconut. Allow to set, then chill until hard.

Beat the butter in a bowl to soften, then gradually add the icing sugar, a large tablespoon at a time, until it is all mixed in. Add the rum with the last spoonful of icing sugar.

Peel the paper away from the cake and slice it horizontally through the middle. Spread about a quarter of the buttercream over the base. Put the other layer on top, then lift on to a cake plate. Cover with the remaining buttercream.

Roughly break the white chocolate bark into shards, peeling it away from the paper. Position on the outside of the cake. Sprinkle the middle of the cake with coconut to finish.

SANTA HATS

A must for a Christmas tea! Hiding underneath the fluffy rim of Santa's hat is a delicate lemon sponge. You could also use clementine or orange zest instead of the lemon if you prefer. Freeze any leftover bits of sponge and save for a trifle.

MAKES 10

60g butter, at room temperature, plus extra
  for greasing
60g golden caster sugar
1 medium egg, beaten
60g self-raising flour
zest of ½ a lemon
200ml double cream
1 tbsp icing sugar
10 strawberries
desiccated coconut, for sprinkling

Preheat the oven to 180°C/160°C fan/gas 4. Butter a 16.5–17cm shallow round baking tin and line with greaseproof paper.

Beat the butter and sugar together in a bowl using an electric hand whisk, or a wooden spoon if you fancy firming up the bingo wings. Gradually beat in the egg. Sift over the flour, then fold in with the lemon zest. Spoon into the tin and spread evenly over the base in a thin layer. Bake for 20–25 minutes, until golden. Take the cake out of the oven and upturn on to a wire rack to cool.

Beat the double cream and icing sugar in a bowl until just thick.

Peel the greaseproof paper away from the base of the cake, then put on a board. Use a 4cm round cutter or the base of a piping nozzle to stamp out 10 rounds of cake.

Spread the cream all over the round bases, then top each one with a strawberry. Sprinkle the coconut around the base, pushing it up on to the sides with a knife. Put a blob of cream on top of the strawberry to mimic the fluffy bobble on Santa's hat, and sprinkle with coconut.

HEALTHY FRUIT PLATE

A refreshing breakfast to share, featuring a kiwi fruit Christmas tree, banana snowmen and yogurt snow. This makes a sharing plate to serve two or double the ingredients to serve four.

SERVES 2

For the tree
a piece of blackcurrant fruit leather
2–3 kiwi fruit
a few dried cranberries
1 apple
2–3 tbsp natural yogurt
½ a mandarin or clementine, peeled and
 cut widthwise

For the snowmen
1 thin banana
1 red apple
1 dried pineapple ring
a few dried cranberries
a few currants
a piece of dried mango

Cut the fruit leather into about 3 strips then fit them together on a plate, arranged vertically to make the trunk of a tree. Peel the kiwi fruit and slice through the centre into thin slivers. Arrange on top of the fruit leather with the seeds facing upwards, in a tree shape, tucking in slivers here and there.

Arrange the dried cranberries over the top of the kiwi fruit to resemble baubles. Cut a piece of apple in the shape of a pot and position at the bottom of the fruit leather trunk. Spoon yogurt at the base, to look like snow. Put the mandarin or clementine half at the top of the tree.

Make the snowman. Cut 3 × 1.5cm-thick rounds from the banana. Arrange the pieces next to each other in a line, then push in a skewer. Cut a cheek from the apple, then cut a large triangle from it. Push the apple triangle in at the top.

HEALTHY FRUIT PLATE CONTINUED

Tear 2 small pieces from a dried pineapple ring. Pinch the pieces together so the top frills out and push the point into each side of the middle banana to make the snowman's arms.

Roll a cranberry into a line to make the snowman's mouth and push into the top banana. Cut 2 slivers from a currant for eyes and push in, then cut a sliver from the dried mango to make a nose.

Do the same again to make another snowman, then arrange both either side of the fruit tree and serve.

GINGERBREAD CHOCOLATE PUDDINGS

Knocking up these fun, yet fancy, puddings is a cinch with a ready-made ginger cake, then you can shape and craft ready-to-roll icing to make red berries and holly leaves and decorate each ball.

MAKES 4

For the puddings
25g butter
25g cocoa powder
50g icing sugar
200g ready-made ginger cake

To decorate
75g milk chocolate
red and green ready-to-roll icing
icing sugar
35g white chocolate
edible iridescent green dust, to decorate

Beat the butter in a bowl to soften it, then gradually add spoonfuls of the cocoa and icing sugar until it's all used up and you've made a creamy buttercream. Beat in 2 teaspoons of boiling water if it feels very dry.

Crumble the ginger cake into the buttercream and stir everything together to make a stiff mixture. Divide roughly into 4 and shape each portion into a round. Flatten off one side so each pudding sits level.

Melt the milk chocolate in a bowl resting over a pan of simmering water, making sure the base doesn't touch the water. Cool for 10 minutes.

Rest the cakes on a wire rack sitting on top of a board or baking sheet. Spoon the melted chocolate all over to cover, then allow to set.

GINGERBREAD CHOCOLATE PUDDINGS
CONTINUED

Pinch a small piece of red ready-to-roll icing and roll into a small ball, like a berry. Do the same with 11 more pieces to make 12 berries.

Roll out a piece of green ready-to-roll icing on a board dusted with a little icing sugar until it's a couple of millimetres thick. Cut out 12 holly leaves and score a line through the middle for the spine.

Now melt the white chocolate in a bowl over a pan of simmering water as before, allowing it to cool for 10 minutes, too. Drizzle over the top to mimic icing. Position the berries on top, followed by the holly leaves between the berries.

If you want to decorate the holly leaves, brush a little edible dust over the top.

CHRISTMAS CAKE PARCELS

A just-for-one cake decorated in glorious technicolour icing in the shape of a present. The cake is a light fruit sponge, flavoured with Christmas spices. It can be made up to a week before decorating, wrapped in cling film and kept cool in an airtight container, or frozen for up to a month.

MAKES 9 MINI CAKES

75g sultanas
75g currants, chopped
75g dried apricots, chopped
75ml whisky
175g butter, at room temperature, plus extra
  for greasing
175g light muscovado sugar
3 large eggs, beaten
100g self-raising flour
75g self-raising wholemeal flour
1 teaspoon ground ginger
1 teaspoon ground mixed spice
½ tsp ground cloves
½ tsp ground cinnamon
1 carrot, grated
50g stem ginger in syrup, grated
2 tbsp milk

To decorate
4–6 tbsp apricot glaze
454g pack of marzipan
icing sugar, for dusting
contrasting colours of ready-to-roll icing

CHRISTMAS CAKE PARCELS CONTINUED

Preheat the oven to 150°C/130°C fan/gas 2. Butter a 20cm square cake tin and line with greaseproof paper.

Put the dried fruit into a pan with the whisky and bring to the boil. Simmer for 1 minute, then take off the heat. The fruit will have plumped up and all the liquid will have been absorbed.

Beat the butter and sugar together in a bowl with an electric hand whisk until the mixture has turned a slightly paler colour and looks creamy. Gradually beat in the eggs.

Sift over the flours and spices, then fold in with the carrot, stem ginger, milk and soaked fruit. Mix well, then spoon into the cake tin. Bake in the oven for 2 hours, until a skewer inserted into the centre comes out clean.

Cool in the tin for 20 minutes, then turn out on to a wire rack and allow to cool completely. The cake will keep well, wrapped in cling film, in an airtight container for up to a week.

Trim 1–2cm off each edge to neaten, then cut the cake vertically into 3, then horizontally to make 9 squares. Brush 5 sides of each cake with the apricot glaze. Chop the marzipan into 9 × 35–40g pieces and roll each one out on a board lightly dusted with icing sugar to make a rough square large enough to cover each cube of cake. Cover each cake cube, leaving the unglazed side uncovered – this will be the base. Trim to fit. Leave to dry out overnight.

Choose which colour of ready-to-roll icing you're going to use to be the 'paper' part of each parcel and cut out 9 pieces as before, each weighing approximately 35–40g. Roll out with a little icing sugar, taking care not to use too much.

Brush the marzipan with water and carefully place the icing on top. Smooth over and wrap at the edges to make a parcel.

Use contrasting pieces of icing to create plain ribbon, tags or twisted ribbons, cutting, rolling out and shaping as necessary.

CHOCOLATE ROBINS

I've included a template for this cute little bird so that anyone can create these chocolate lollies. If you want to give them as a gift, wrap them in cake pop bags and secure with a twist of ribbon.

MAKES 4

50g milk chocolate
75g white chocolate
10g dark chocolate, around 80% cocoa solids
red food colouring paste

You will need
4 lolly sticks

Trace the robin template (overleaf) 4 times on to a sheet of baking parchment, then turn the paper over and put on a white board so you can see the outline.

Melt the milk chocolate in a bowl set over a pan of simmering water, making sure the base doesn't touch the water. Take the bowl off the pan and set aside for 10 minutes.

Melt the white chocolate in the same way, then take the bowl off the pan and set aside for 15 minutes to cool.

Spoon the milk chocolate on to the top part of the robin template, then fill in the rest of the shape with the white chocolate. Push the lolly sticks into the white chocolate part, then drizzle more white chocolate over the top. Allow to cool, then chill until set.

CHOCOLATE ROBINS CONTINUED

Melt the dark chocolate in the same way and draw the eye and beak on to the shape. Allow this to set again.

Colour each robin's breast in red, using a small brush, flicking the colour so that it looks like feathers.

ROBIN TEMPLATE ×4

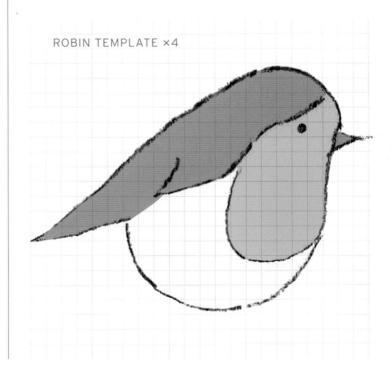

REINDEER DONUTS

Take a box of ready-made mini donuts and transform them simply and easily into Santa's herd of reindeer with just a handful of sweet ingredients.

MAKES 9

100g milk or dark chocolate
9 mini ring donuts
a tube of Smarties
a bag of mini pretzels
mini marshmallows

Line a baking tray with baking parchment and rest a wire rack over the top.

Melt the chocolate in a bowl resting over a pan of simmering water, making sure the base doesn't touch the water. Take the bowl off the pan and allow to cool for 10–15 minutes.

Place the donuts on top of the rack and carefully spoon chocolate over each one. Allow to set for 5 minutes, then push a sweet into the middle. Break the pretzels to shape into antlers, or leave them whole if you prefer, and push into the top of each donut. Cut eyes from the marshmallows and push into the top.

Cook's tip
If you want to label each donut, spoon leftover chocolate into a piping bag fitted with a fine nozzle and pipe the names of Santa's deer on to baking parchment. Leave to cool, then peel off and set near each treat.

MERINGUE BAUBLES

These make the perfect Christmas food gift. Bag up into parcels of cellophane and tie with a pretty ribbon. If you're serving them at home, arrange on a plate with a bowl of whipped sweetened cream, swirled with cranberry jelly.

MAKES ABOUT 50

2 large egg whites
caster sugar (see method)
edible dust in silver, gold, pink and purple

Preheat the oven to 110ºC/90ºC fan/gas ½. Line a baking sheet with baking parchment.

Weigh the egg whites, note the weight, then double it and measure that quantity of caster sugar.

Whisk the egg whites in a spotlessly clean, grease-free bowl until firm and the beaten whites don't move around in the bowl. At this stage, you should be able to hold the bowl upside down above your head and the mixture won't slip around or fall out.

Gradually add the sugar, a tablespoon at a time, and whisk in until the mixture is smooth and glossy.

MERINGUE BAUBLES CONTINUED

Spoon into a piping bag fitted with a 1cm round nozzle. Pipe little rounds on to the parchment, lifting the nozzle up quickly to make a loop at the top and create a bauble shape. Bake in the oven for around 50 minutes, until they easily lift from the paper.

Turn off the oven and leave the meringues inside to cool for an hour. Store in an airtight container for up to 2 weeks.

ARCTIC SCENE

This may look like a festive Blue Peter challenge, but it's easy to create this centrepiece with a few simple instructions. The penguins' bodies are made from home-made marzipan, then covered with coloured ready-to-roll icing and the scene set by building an igloo from a box of sugar cubes. Once the penguin figures are made and covered with icing, they'll keep well in an airtight box for up to two weeks.

MAKES 8

For the marzipan bodies
40g hazelnuts
60g ground almonds
50g golden caster sugar
50g golden icing sugar
2–3 tbsp beaten egg

To decorate
1 pack of black ready-to-roll icing
1 pack of white ready-to-roll icing
1 pack of orange ready-to-roll icing
coloured icing to make scarves, hats, earmuffs

Roughly chop the hazelnuts, then whiz in a food processor until finely ground. Tip into a bowl and add the ground almonds, both types of sugar and the beaten egg. Mix everything together to make a paste. Shape into a round, wrap in cling film and chill.

To make the body of each penguin, divide the marzipan into 8 even-sized pieces. Roll one into an oval, around the size of an apricot. Tap one end on a board several times, to flatten. Do the same with the other 7 pieces, then chill for 15 minutes to firm up.

Pinch off 8 small pieces of black icing (around 12g each) and roll each into a round ball to make a head. Next, pinch off 8 pieces, each around 6g in weight, and roll each out thinly. Shape into a large triangle. Brush three-quarters of each marzipan body with water and wrap the icing around to make the penguin's coat, trimming and shaping to fit.

To make the penguin's white bib, take a small piece of white icing and roll out on a board. Cut out 8 triangular shapes to fit the uncovered part of the body and cover the remaining marzipan. Again, you may need to trim this to fit. Wet the top of each body and push the head on top.

Roll out small balls for eyes in the black icing, then use the orange icing to shape the beak and feet. Use any leftover black icing to shape the wings. At this stage, you can get creative with the positions of the penguins.

Roll out a little more white icing and cut out 8 small heart shapes for the penguins' faces. Wet the back of the icing and stick on the front of the head of each penguin. Decorate with the eyes, beak and feet.

Now get creative with the other colours and shape earmuffs, hats and scarves to accessorize each penguin.

Cook's tip
To create an Arctic scene, roll out enough white ready-to-roll icing to cover a large plate or board. Build an igloo with white sugar cubes and roll any leftover white icing into balls for snowballs. Make a pool in the ice by painting a puddle shape in blue edible ink and colouring it in. Make a fish by kneading together a little white icing with black icing and shaping into its form. Put in the pool. Sit the penguins on the Arctic scene and arrange as the centrepiece.

SNOWY HOT CHOCOLATE

This indulgent drink, sharpened with a slug of brandy and a sprinkling of spice to cut through the richness, is a wonderful way to warm up after a long winter walk.

SERVES 4

75g dark chocolate, at least 70% cocoa solids,
  chopped
500ml milk
2 tsp mixed spice
2 tbsp brandy
200ml double cream
2 tsp golden icing sugar
edible silver stars

Put the chocolate into a large jug. Pour the milk into a pan, add the spice and brandy and bring to the boil. Pour immediately over the chocolate and stir well. Return to the pan and bring to a simmer.

Whip the double cream in a bowl with the icing sugar. Divide the hot chocolate between 4 glasses and spoon the cream on top. Sprinkle with the silver stars and serve.

Cook's tip
Hot chocolate makes a great present. Just chop 300g of dark chocolate, then whiz in a blender until finely chopped. Stir in 2 tablespoons of mixed spice and spoon into a bag or jar. Wrap up with the cooking instructions above and give with a bottle of brandy.

WHITE CHOCOLATE BOMBE

There's no need for an ice-cream machine in this easy-to-make recipe. Whisking egg whites, double cream and an egg yolk and sugar mixture creates the light-as-air texture.

SERVES 6

150g mixed dried fruit, such as apricots, golden
   cherries, pineapple, papaya
50g desiccated coconut
4 tbsp Malibu
3 medium eggs, separated
100g golden caster sugar
300ml double cream
50g white chocolate, grated

To decorate
50g white chocolate
a selection of dried fruit, such as apricots,
   golden cherries, pineapple, papaya
edible gold dust

Line a 900ml pudding bowl with cling film.

Chop the dried fruit into small pieces and put into a pan with the desiccated coconut and Malibu. Bring to the boil and simmer for 1 minute. Then turn off the heat and set aside to macerate.

Whisk the egg whites in a spotlessly clean, grease-free bowl. Whisk in 25g of sugar, then set aside. In a separate bowl, whisk the egg yolks and remaining caster sugar until pale, thick and moussey. Lightly whip the cream in another bowl until it's a similar consistency to the egg yolk mixture.

WHITE CHOCOLATE BOMBE CONTINUED

Fold the cream into the egg yolk mixture gently. Add a tablespoon of the whisked egg white and fold in, then fold in the remainder. Spoon into a freezeproof container, cover and freeze for an hour. Stir the hardened edges into the middle and freeze again for another hour. Fold in the macerated fruit and grated white chocolate, then spoon into the lined pudding bowl and cover and freeze again for 5 hours, until firm.

To decorate, melt the white chocolate in a bowl resting over a pan of simmering water, ensuring the base doesn't touch the water.

Take the pudding out of the freezer, unwrap and upturn on to a plate. Drizzle over the white chocolate, then arrange the whole dried fruit on top. Dust with a little edible gold dust and serve.

CHERRY PANDORO STAR

Pandoro, the light Italian cake shaped in a star, forms the base of this showstopping dessert. If you can get hold of good fresh cherries, use those, or buy a jar of good-quality preserved cherries.

SERVES 6

250g tub of mascarpone
1 tbsp kirsch, plus extra to drizzle
zest and juice of 1 orange
2 tbsp icing sugar, plus extra for dusting
500g Italian pandoro cake
200g fresh cherries, or a jar of preserved
  cherries, drained

In a bowl, beat together the mascarpone, kirsch, orange zest, juice and icing sugar.

Slice the pandoro horizontally 3 times, to make 4 thick star-shaped slices. Put one slice on a plate, drizzle over a little kirsch, then spoon over a quarter of the mascarpone mixture, spreading it all over the cake.

Repeat this twice more, twisting each slice of the star slightly to expose each point on the one below. Put the top of the cake on top and spoon over the remaining mascarpone mixture.

Push a cherry into each point on the cake, then pile a handful in the centre. Dust with icing sugar and serve.

ORANGE SNOWFLAKE CAKES

It takes a steady hand and a keen eye to draw the snowflake meringue shapes on to the parchment, but after you've done a couple you'll easily get the hang of it. They're very delicate shapes, so take care when removing them from the paper – use a palette knife to slide under each one to release.

MAKES 12

For the snowflake meringues
1 medium egg white
caster sugar (see method)

For the cakes
150g butter
150g golden caster sugar
2 large eggs
150g self-raising flour
zest of 1 orange

For the topping
250g mascarpone
60g icing sugar

Preheat the oven to 110ºC/90ºC/gas ½. Line a baking sheet with baking parchment.

First, make the meringue decoration. Weigh the egg white. Note the weight and double it, then weigh out this amount of caster sugar.

Put the egg white into a clean, grease-free bowl and whisk until the mixture is stiff and doesn't move around in the bowl. Whisk in the caster sugar, a little at a time, until the mixture is smooth and shiny.

Secure the parchment on the baking sheet by dotting a little raw meringue underneath each corner of the piece and sticking it back on to the sheet.

Spoon the meringue into a piping bag fitted with a 2mm nozzle and pipe at least 12 snowflake shapes on to it. Bake in the oven for 1½–2 hours, until the meringue comes away easily from the parchment.

ORANGE SNOWFLAKE CAKES CONTINUED

When the meringues have cooked, take out of
the oven and cool on a wire rack. Turn up the
oven to 180°C/160°C fan/gas 4. Line a bun tin
with paper cases.

Beat the butter and sugar together in a bowl
until soft and creamy. Gradually add the eggs,
adding a tablespoon of flour if the mixture
is curdling. Fold in the remaining flour and
orange zest.

Spoon between the cases and bake for 15–20
minutes until golden. Transfer to a wire rack
to cool.

Fold the mascarpone and icing sugar together
and use to ice each cake. Top with a meringue
snowflake and serve.

CHOUX PASTRY WREATHS

A ring of choux makes the ideal edible wreath. Fill with a light-as-air cream, then decorate with a thin glacé icing, flaked almonds and dried cranberries.

SERVES 4

For the choux pastry
60g plain flour
40g butter
1 large egg, beaten

For the filling
2 tbsp cornflour
3 medium egg yolks
75g golden caster sugar, plus 1 tbsp
300ml milk
225ml double cream

To decorate
4 tbsp golden icing sugar, plus extra for dusting
8 pecan nuts
4 dried cranberries

Preheat the oven to 200°C/180°C fan/gas 6. Draw 4 × 9cm rounds, using a ramekin or pot, on to a piece of baking parchment. Turn the parchment over and put on a baking sheet.

Sift the flour twice, then sift it one more time on to a sheet of greaseproof paper.

Put the butter into a pan with 110ml water. Place the pan over a gentle heat to allow the butter to melt. As soon as it has melted, turn up the heat to bring the mixture to a rolling boil. Take the pan off the heat and pour in the flour from the greaseproof. Beat well with a wooden spoon until the mixture forms a ball. Set aside to cool for a few minutes.

Add the egg a little at a time to the mixture and continue to beat in until the mixture is smooth and glossy.

Spoon into a piping bag fitted with a 1cm nozzle. Pipe around the traced rounds. Bake in the oven for around 20 minutes, until golden and puffed up. Make a small hole in the side of each where it naturally cracks to let out the steam and continue to bake for 1–2 minutes more. Transfer to a wire rack to cool.

CHOUX PASTRY WREATHS CONTINUED

Now make the filling. Stir the cornflour, egg yolks, 50g of sugar and 2 tablespoons of milk into a bowl. Pour the rest of the milk into a pan and bring to the boil. As soon as it has come to the boil, pour it over the cornflour mixture and stir well. Return to a clean pan and bring to the boil. Allow to simmer for 2–3 minutes until thickened. Scrape into a bowl and allow to cool.

Whip the cream with the remaining tablespoon of sugar in a separate bowl until thick. Gently fold into the cooled custard. Split the choux buns in half horizontally and pipe the mixture over the base of each, using a 1.5cm star nozzle.

Stir about 1 teaspoon of water into the icing sugar to make a smooth icing. Drizzle over each choux wreath. Push 2 pecan nuts and a dried cranberry into the top of each one, and dust lightly with icing sugar.

Fondest Greetings
for Your Happiness

Joyeux Noël !

SAVOURY

SANTA'S SAVOURY SLEIGH

A fun alternative to the ubiquitous gingerbread house. This is made from home-made cracker dough, baked in the shape of a sleigh, and filled with Baby Bel cheese presents.

SERVES ABOUT 4

For the dough
100g plain flour, plus a little extra
100g wholemeal flour
25g oats
1 tsp salt
1 tbsp olive oil
1 egg, beaten
sesame and poppy seeds, for sprinkling

To stick the parts together
125g royal icing sugar

To complete the scene
Baby Bel cheeses
sticks of celery

You will need
the template overleaf, cut out in cardboard

Put the flours, oats and salt into a food processor and whiz to finely chop the oats. Tip into a bowl. Make a well in the centre and pour in the olive oil and 100ml of water. Stir the mixture with a table knife to make a soft dough.

Roll out the dough between 2 sheets of baking parchment until about 2mm thick. Take off the top sheet of baking parchment and use the templates overleaf to cut around and make both sides of the sleigh, plus the base. Transfer to a baking sheet lined with parchment.

Roll out the remaining dough and use to make about 20 small square crackers.

Prick all the pieces of dough all over with a fork and chill for 15 minutes. Preheat the oven to 180°C/160°C fan/gas 4.

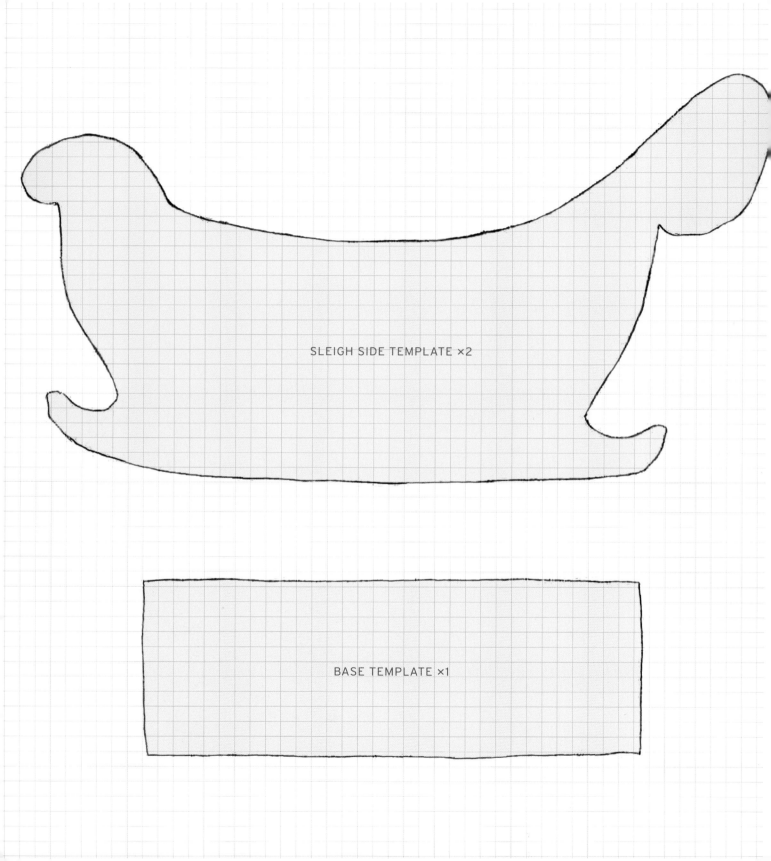

SLEIGH SIDE TEMPLATE ×2

BASE TEMPLATE ×1

Brush around the edge of each side of the sleigh with egg and sprinkle with the seeds. Bake in the oven for around 40–45 minutes until golden. Put the crackers on a separate baking sheet and cook for around 20–25 minutes, until baked. Cool both on a wire rack.

Sift the royal icing sugar into a bowl. Add 20ml of water and whisk with an electric hand whisk for 5 minutes. Spoon into a piping bag and snip a fine point at the end. Drizzle a thin line of icing along the bottom of one edge of one sleigh, leaving a border of about 0.5cm. Lie it on its side, then put the longest edge of the base along the paste and press down. Prop it up and allow to set. Once set, do the same on the other side to construct the sleigh.

Put the sleigh on a plate. Tie ribbons around each individual cheese and push the celery sticks into a small glass. Stack the crackers next to it and serve.

PORK, THYME AND APRICOT CHRISTMAS PIES

A savoury alternative to a fruit-filled mince pie. The crisp pastry encasing the pork and fruit filling is rich and flavoursome, enriched with cream cheese, double cream and herbs.

MAKES 4

For the pastry
225g plain flour, sifted
85g butter, chilled and diced
25g cream cheese
2 tbsp double cream
½ tsp salt
½ tsp dried mixed herbs
1 egg, beaten

For the filling
10g butter
½ tbsp olive oil
½ onion, finely chopped
½ celery stick, finely chopped
the leaves from a small handful of thyme
100g pork mince
1 small apple, grated
10g dried apricots, finely chopped

For the pastry, put the flour into a food processor and add the butter, cream cheese, double cream, salt and herbs. Whiz to mix everything together. Drizzle over 2 tablespoons of water and whiz again. Tip into a bowl and bring the mixture together with your hands, then knead lightly until smooth. Wrap in greaseproof paper and chill for 15 minutes.

For the filling, melt the butter in a pan with the oil. As soon as the butter has melted, stir in the onion and celery and cook over a low heat for about 10 minutes until softened. Tip into a bowl and cool. Add the remaining filling ingredients, season and mix well.

Preheat the oven to 200ºC/180ºC fan/gas 6.

Divide the pastry into 3. Roll out one third on a lightly floured board and stamp out 12 rounds, using a 7cm cutter. Push into a lightly greased 12-hole bun tin. Spoon the pork mince mixture evenly between the rounds.

PORK, THYME AND APRICOT CHRISTMAS PIES CONTINUED

Roll out another third of the pastry and stamp out another 12 rounds using a 7cm cutter. Brush the edge of each filled pastry round with beaten egg, then top with the lid.

Roll out the remaining pastry and cut out stars, bells and holly leaves. Brush the beaten egg all over the pies and arrange the decorations on top, then brush again.

Bake in the oven for 20–25 minutes until golden. Serve warm.

OLIVE AND TOMATO STARS

These dainty stars are cut from simple squares of puff pastry, with the corners folded in to create the shape. Serve topped with cream cheese and a green olive or tomato tapenade.

MAKES AROUND 40

½ × 375g ready-rolled sheet of puff pastry
50g green olives
leaves from a few thyme sprigs
olive oil
50g sun-dried tomatoes
a little grated lemon zest
25g parmesan cheese, finely grated
100g cream cheese

Preheat the oven to 200ºC/180ºC fan/gas 6.

Unroll the puff pastry on a board and cut into 40 × 3cm squares. Cut down each corner diagonally into the square, leaving a small circle in the middle. Fold one corner of each down into the middle and press to secure. Transfer to a non-stick baking sheet and chill for 10 minutes.

Whiz the green olives in a mini food processor with the thyme leaves and 1 teaspoon of olive oil until blended. Scrape into a bowl and set aside. Do the same with the sun-dried tomatoes and lemon zest.

Sprinkle the stars with a little grated parmesan and season. Bake the puff pastry stars in the oven for 10–15 minutes, until golden. Transfer to a wire rack to cool.

Spoon or pipe some cream cheese into the middle of each star and top with a little green tapenade or sun-dried tomato tapenade. Garnish with a few extra thyme leaves.

MINI BAKED POTATO BAUBLES

Quick canapés, which can be rustled up in minutes with the minimum of fuss, are a cook's dream around Christmas. These look stunning, yet are very simple to prepare. For vegetarians, use a vegetarian caviar or finely chop a marinated red pepper and spoon a little on top.

SERVES 4-6

20 baby new potatoes
2 tsp olive oil
salt
soured cream
salmon caviar
chives, freshly chopped

Preheat the oven to 200°C/180°C fan/gas 6.

Cut a cross in the top of each new potato and put into a roasting tin. Drizzle with the oil and season with salt. Use a spoon to toss the potatoes in the oil to coat them evenly. Roast for 30–40 minutes.

Remove from the oven and cool for 5 minutes. Spoon the soured cream on top, followed by the caviar and a sprinkling of chopped chives.

SPICY DUCHESSE POTATO CHRISTMAS TREES

Soft pillowy mashed potato is hidden inside a crisp shell in these bite-size treats. Serve as canapés or as part of a meal. They're topped with a herb dressing and a pinch of chilli for a spicy kick.

SERVES 4 (MAKES ABOUT 20)

300g potatoes, chopped
a good pinch of salt
½ a medium egg
25g butter
25ml milk
5g parmesan cheese, freshly grated

To decorate
10g parsley
10g basil
4 tbsp olive oil
a good squeeze of lemon juice
salt and freshly ground black pepper
crushed chilli flakes

Put the potatoes into a pan and cover with cold water. Add a pinch of salt, put a lid on the pan and bring to the boil. Turn down the heat and simmer for about 15 minutes, until the potatoes are tender.

Drain well, then mash the potato using a potato ricer to make a really smooth mash. Beat in the egg, butter, milk and parmesan.

Spoon the mash into a piping bag fitted with a 1–2cm star nozzle. Preheat the oven to 220ºC/200ºC fan/gas 7 and line a baking sheet with baking parchment.

Keeping the nozzle quite close to the parchment, squeeze the potato out on to the baking sheet until you've shaped a thick base, around 3cm in width. Continue to squeeze, gradually pulling the bag up until you make the shape of a Christmas tree. Make sure you don't pull the nozzle up too quickly, otherwise you'll end up with a long thin tree!

SPICY DUCHESSE POTATO CHRISTMAS TREES
CONTINUED

Bake for about 18 minutes, until golden.

Whiz the herbs, oil, lemon juice and seasoning in a mini food processor to make a herby dressing. When the potatoes come out of the oven, drizzle a little of the herb dressing over each one and sprinkle over a few crushed chilli flakes for a festive feel.

CANAPÉ WREATH

A fun way to serve nibbles: arrange sprigs of rosemary in a round, then garnish with spoonfuls of olives, gherkins and caperberries and sacks of mini peppers filled with herby cream cheese.

SERVES 6

lots of rosemary sprigs
50g cream cheese
2 tbsp freshly chopped herbs, such as parsley,
   lemon thyme and chives
8–10 Peppadew peppers
around 75g bocconcini (little mozzarellas)
extra virgin olive oil
crushed chilli flakes
1–2 marinated peppers from a jar
around 200g mixed olives
8 caperberries
8 gherkins, halved
2 slices of lemon
balsamic vinegar

Arrange the rosemary on a large round plate or board in a wreath shape, around 20cm across, and spritz well with cold water.

Beat together the cream cheese and herbs in a bowl, then spoon into the Peppadew peppers. Transfer to a plate and chill.

Put the bocconcini into a bowl with 1 teaspoon of extra virgin olive oil and a good pinch of chilli flakes. Toss to coat in the mixture, then chill.

Slice the marinated peppers into thin strips. Shape each one into a bow, as pictured, cutting as need be to shape the loops and the tails of the ribbon.

Assemble the wreath: portion the olives into 3, then spoon at even spots over the wreath. Do the same with the caperberries and gherkins. Then start to dress the empty parts of the wreath with the other bits: the cheesy peppadew peppers, the red pepper bows and the bocconcini. Cut each lemon slice up to the middle, then twist and arrange on the rosemary.

Mix together 1 tablespoon each of extra virgin olive oil and balsamic vinegar and season well. Drizzle over the olives, caperberries and gherkins, then serve.

SPICED POPCORN HANGINGS

Hang jars of this subtly spiced popcorn on the tree or around the house. They also make the ideal food gift.

MAKES 6–8 JARS

1 tsp sea salt
½ tsp freshly ground black pepper
a good couple of pinches of chilli flakes
½ tsp ground coriander
½ tsp cayenne pepper
1 tsp golden caster sugar
1 tbsp olive oil
100g popping corn
a large knob of butter

You will need
6–8 round jars and ribbon

Mix together the salt, pepper, spices and sugar.

Heat the oil in a large pan over a medium to high heat. There needs to be enough room in there for the corn kernels to pop and puff up.

Add the corn and cover with a lid. Continue to cook, shaking the pan every now and then, and after about 10 seconds the corn will start to pop. Turn the heat down slightly and continue to cook until all the corn has popped.

Take off the lid and add the butter and spice mixture. Put the lid back on the pan and shake well to mix everything together. Divide among the jars and seal with a lid, then tie with a ribbon.

CAMEMBERT PARCEL

A sharing puff pastry bundle of melted cheese. Serve with a pot of cranberry sauce and a crisp salad to cut through the richness.

MAKES 1 PARCEL, SERVES 4

½ × 375g sheet ready-rolled puff pastry
a little plain flour, for rolling out
250g Camembert wheel
1 medium egg, beaten

Unroll the pastry on a board lightly dusted with a little plain flour.

Cut a 1cm length off each edge so you have 4 strips left over. Take the cheese out of its box and wrapping and place in the middle of the pastry. Wrap each edge around, trimming the pastry if there's any excess, then turn it over and put on a plate. Brush the pastry all over with the beaten egg.

Trim 2 pieces of the leftover pastry and wrap over the top of the parcel to resemble ribbon. Arrange the remaining pastry bits on top, shaped in a bow.

Chill for 15 minutes. Preheat the oven to 220°C/200°C fan/gas 7. Put a baking sheet in to heat up.

Take the parcel out of the fridge and brush over the eggwash again. Slide on to the hot baking sheet and bake for 20–25 minutes, until the pastry is golden.

CHEESE AND CHARCUTERIE JINGLE BELL

Knock up this plate of nibbles in an instant and serve on a contrasting gold platter for the maximum effect.

SERVES 6

60g Cheddar cheese
50g Red Leicester cheese
30g Wensleydale and cranberry cheese
8–12 pieces of salami
6 pieces of coppa
6 baby plum tomatoes

You will need
cocktail sticks

Take the cheese and cured meat out of the fridge about 20 minutes before serving to take off the chill.

Cut all the cheese into 1cm pieces.

Arrange the salami in a curve at the bottom of a large serving platter, leaving space at the bottom to put a shot glass or small pot.

Put the coppa above the curve, followed by the plum tomatoes. Next arrange the Cheddar, slicing a couple of the pieces in half to make triangles to neaten the sides of the bell. Do the same with the Red Leicester and finally finish with the Wensleydale and cranberry cheese.

Fill the glass or pot with cocktail sticks and serve.

TEAR-AND-SHARE CHRISTMAS ROLLS

Make a special breakfast with this combination of white, wholemeal and granary rolls baked in a Christmas tree shape. Serve with a pepper herb butter alongside scrambled eggs and crisp rashers of bacon.

SERVES 6-8

For the white rolls
½ tsp dried active yeast
½ tsp sugar
200g strong white bread flour
½ tsp salt
1 tsp olive oil

For the wholemeal rolls
As above, replacing the 200g strong white bread flour with 200g wholemeal bread flour

For the seeded rolls
As above, replacing the 200g strong white bread flour with 200g granary bread flour
Plus add 1 tbsp mixed seeds, such as linseed, poppy and sesame

For a red pepper butter
100g marinated peppers from a jar
100g sun-dried tomatoes
75g softened butter

TEAR-AND-SHARE CHRISTMAS ROLLS
CONTINUED

First make the white rolls. Put the yeast and sugar into a small bowl. Add 150ml of warm water and set aside to activate for 5 minutes. Sift the flour and salt into a large bowl. Make a well in the centre and pour in the olive oil, followed by the yeast mixture. Stir well to make a soft, craggy dough, then knead on a board for about 10 minutes, until smooth and elastic. Put into a clean bowl, cover and put in a warm place for 30 minutes.

Repeat this method twice more to make the other two doughs.

Preheat the oven to 190°C/170°C fan/gas 5. Line a large baking sheet with baking parchment. Split each dough into 6–8 balls, depending on the size of your baking sheet. Roll each into a round and arrange alternately on the baking sheet into the shape of a large triangle to look like a Christmas tree. If you have any dough left over, you can stamp out star shapes using a small cutter and bake on a separate baking sheet. Leave to prove for 10 minutes. Bake in the oven for 40–50 minutes, until the buns sound hollow when tapped lightly on the top. Transfer to a wire rack to cool.

Roughly chop the marinated pepper and sun-dried tomatoes and put into a blender with the butter. Season well and whiz until smooth. Serve with the rolls.

Cook's tip
These little rolls are also delicious with a smoked salmon butter. To make it, whiz 250g of smoked salmon and 75g of softened butter in a food processor to combine. Stir in a small handful of chopped herbs and a squeeze of lemon juice. Season to taste.

Special thanks to Caroline for the lovely commission;
Fran and Dan for all their help along the way; Sarah for the
photos; Alice for the gorgeous prop styling; Trish Burgess
for the edit; Anna for the design; Kevan Westbury for
taste-testing; Martha for drawing the robin template and
Ellie for her invaluable help in the kitchen. This book
is in celebration of Flora, born on Christmas Day.